The S2P2

Communication Styles Survey
for Leaders

Stephanie Phillips & Patrick Sanaghan

"It is simply impossible to become a great leader without being a great communicator—not a great talker"

– Mike Myatt

Published by: COURAGELAND PUBLISHING
                 168 East State Street
                 Doylestown, PA 18901

ISBN 978-1-61014-461-2

Introduction

Effective communication is one of the essential skills every leader needs in order lead their people well. (Myatt, 2012; Groysberg & Slind, 2012; Gleeson, 2016; Burgoon, Guerrero & Floyd, 2016; Ming Chng, Yeol-Kim, Gilbreath & Andersson,2018). Unfortunately, too many leaders are poor communicators (Sanaghan & Eberbach, 2013 2016; Heifetz & Linsky, 2017; Zugaro & Zugaro, 2017).

We've had the opportunity of working with hundreds of leaders in higher education; the non-profit world; government; and corporate sectors over the past decade. There have been many great communicators and a whole lot of poor ones. The problem is that most leaders think that they are excellent communicators, but unfortunately many are not.

One of the authors has worked with over 2,500 leaders to review there 360-degree feedback instruments in coaching sessions. In our conversations with these leaders, it was striking that almost all of them put "excellent communicator" in the top five or six leadership skills that they believed they possessed. The *anonymous* and honest responses from their people were often not in agreement with how these leaders saw themselves.

When we talk to leaders about communication, they tend to focus solely on their own verbal communication skills. The ability to be articulate, quick on your feet, inspiring—even "charming"—are the descriptors many use to define good communication. Yet the ability to listen is an equally important communication skill that it is often cited by followers, and a weak spot for many leaders (Heifetz & Linsky, 2017; Sanaghan & Eberbach, 2013; Zugaro & Zugaro, 2017).

Communication can get rather complex and complicated quickly. It can involve written communication; the ability to listen well; verbal communication; visual communication; and nonverbal communication. Our survey focuses on *verbal communication styles* only.

As you will see, we will use some behavioral descriptions to provide a "picture" of what a certain communication style might look like. For example:

A. One of the communication styles in the survey is "Methodical" which describes someone who is very detail-orientated and prefers facts to expressing feelings. They can bereserved in group discussions, and often get caught with analysis paralysis and lost in the details of a conversation. These types of leaders don't "wing it" and come well- prepared to meetings and conversations.

B. A second communication style, the "Decisive," is assertive in conversations and discussions and they often speaks rather fast. They feel comfortable freely sharing their opinions, ideas, and love debating the issues. They are practical kinds of leaders who drive towards actions and solutions. They are interested in bottom-line thinking and tend notto like conversations that wander all over the place.

You get the idea. Describing the behavioral aspects of each communication style helps us understand what it looks like in real life.

Communication Note: For readers who want to learn more about the power and complexity of *nonverbal communication,* we suggest reading *Nonverbal Communication* (Burgoon, Guerrero & Floyd, 2016). It is an excellent resource.

Although we use many resources and references in this survey, it is not intended to be academic in tone or tenor. This is a "commonsensical" assessment that is friendly and easy to comprehend for the layperson. It will provide any leaders with practical insight into the ways they communicate with others.

Most importantly, it will share ideas and strategies for effectively communicating with others who have a **different** communication style than yours; sharing insights about how you communicate when you are under stress; and suggesting strategies to consider when you have conflict with different styles.

Some clear points to consider as a leader:

A. Most everything happens with a conversation. If you can't communicate effectively with others, you simply cannot lead them effectively. This does not mean being a great public speaker—we have way too many of those—and they still can't lead. Mainly because they talk way too much or their people don't trust them (Lee, 2017; Hurley, 2010)

   Conversations can be with individuals, small and large groups, and are one of the most effective ways to influence others. Developing your communication skills is an ongoing journey for any leader. Hopefully this survey will provide helpful information about your current communication style.

B. You can't *not* communicate because you are communicating always, whether you intend to or not. People are always watching their leaders for signals. These could be: the way a leader responds to feedback or contrary opinions; how well and honestly they answer a tough question; *(people's baloney detectors are surprisingly keen)*; and how well they listen to others (Doty, 2016; Sanaghan, 2016). Never forget this: you are never *not* the leader and people are looking all the time. What's your communication-style message? Do you know what it is?

   If not, then you have no idea about your communication intentions, versus your actual impact on others. This can leave you blind and clueless, which is a dangerous place for any leader to be. Deeply understanding how effectively you communicate with others is a valuable asset for every leader

C. The ability to communicate effectively, influence followers *authentically*, (no manipulation), and create shared meaning is at the heart of leadership (Heifetz & Linsky, 2017; Perlmutter, 2018). People need to believe in their leader's competence and character, or that person simply cannot lead them (Sanaghan & Eberbach, 2016; Ming Chng, Yeol-Kim, Gilbreath & Andersson, 2018).

Communication with all its complex nuances is *the* essential vehicle to connect with people, and engage and attract followers. Every leader needs to understand how others communicate and see their world (Groysberg & Slind, 2012; Scisco, Biech & Hallenbeck, 2017). The only way to understand others is through communication, conversation, and listening.

Communication Note: One of the very best resources for interested readers is "COMPASS: Your Guide for Leadership Development & Coaching" (Scisco, Biech & Hallenbeck, 2017). This large volume is published by the Center for Creative Leadership, one of the most outstanding resources for leadership in the world. They identify the "Fundamental Four Competencies" for effective leadership as: 1**) Communication**; 2) Influence; 3) Learning Agility; and 4) Self-Awareness.

The **S2P2** survey is easy to take and will provide you with a description of your strongest communication style or your communication preference. A deep understanding your style will enable you to play to the strengths of your style and be conscious about mitigating your weaknesses. We all have weaknesses regarding our communication style; the key is understanding how your weakness can get in your way, and strategizing how to avoid our communication pitfalls.

You can also use this survey to better understand the diverse communication skills of the members of your team or work group. You will learn through this survey that people communicate *very differently.* The key leadership question then is, *"How do I use our communication differences as assets and not have them become liabilities?"* Leaders need to be able to use the many communication gifts that their people bring to the table, and not let their differences get in the way.

We have worked with hundreds of teams and groups and have found that a team can go downhill quickly when communication breaks down (Sanaghan & Eberbach, 2013). People start making assumptions about each other (usually negative ones), judge other's intentions, and begin to debate the issues rather than using dialogue and inquiry to discuss them. In short, it gets messy and ugly fast.

Later in this monograph we will provide a *Team Diagnostic Meeting Design* that will enable interested users to deploy their team's communication data to better understand each other's strengths, areas of needed development and most importantly, understand the real implications for their team's *overall performance.*

People have found the **S2P2** to be especially helpful in understanding how to work with others who have dramatically different communication styles than their own. Isn't that one of the real challenges that leaders face? We will offer advice on how to communicate effectively with diverse communication styles and build on the differences rather than being polarized by them.

S2P2
Communications Styles

Decisive	**Animated**
Methodical	**Relatable**

Circle the letter that indicates the closest match for your communications style in the quiz below. A scoring grid follows.

1. I am most comfortable expressing my opinion:
    A. In front of a captive audience.
    B. Anytime and anywhere.
    C. When I know I am right.
    D. In a one-on-one conversation.

2. At a large social gathering, I will:
    A. Talk only with the people I know.
    B. Meet as many new people as possible.
    C. Enjoy my close circle of friends.
    D. Talk to the people I came to see and leave.

3. If I disagree with you, I will:
    A. Stay quiet to avoid confronting you.
    B. Tell you that I disagree and why.
    C. Tell you why your idea won't work.
    D. Ask a lot of questions to understand your point of view.

4. When I ask for help, it is because:
    A. I'm usually the one giving help.
    B. I love brainstorming.
    C. I never ask for help because I figure it out myself.
    D. I want to get it done.

5. My strongest communications skill is:
    A. Selling an idea to anyone.
    B. Asking questions until I understand how it is done.
    C. Being direct and quick on my feet.
    D. Letting you know that I value your opinion.

6. When someone comes to me with personal drama, I respond:
    A. Nod and politely redirect them to an upcoming deadline.
    B. Listen and offer sympathy.
    C. Stir it up! I want to hear all about it.
    D. *Ugh.* Don't bother me with petty things.

7. I like to ask provocative questions:
    A. Absolutely. I love a lively conversation.
    B. Yes, I will challenge a wrong decision.
    C. Never, because it may offend someone.
    D. No, I like to stick with an idea that works.

8. When discussing a new project with a team, I like to start with a:
    A. Decision about the best outcome and work backwards from there.
    B. Review of research from similar projects.
    C. Brainstorming session to imagine the possibilities.
    D. Discussion of how everyone will work together to get it done.

9. I react to people when they get emotional by:
    A. Excusing myself as soon as possible.
    B. Letting them vent.
    C. Discussing them for being too dramatic.
    D. Asking questions to understand the cause.

10. When someone suggests a new way of doing things, I will:
    A. Agree to do it if it helps us be more effective.
    B. Agree that it might be better, especially if it improves morale.
    C. Show excitement about how this could improve all the things.
    D. Ask questions to evaluate the risks involved.

11. The easiest way to make me feel uncomfortable when we talk:
    A. Detail thoroughly why something can't be done.
    B. Tell me to slow down.
    C. Interrupt me.
    D. Ask me to change course halfway through a project.

12. I get bored when people talk about:
    A. I rarely get bored when I'm with people.
    B. What's been done before.
    C. Something I'm not involved in.
    D. What they did over the weekend.

13. When I am speaking in public:
    A. I paint a picture of possibilities for people.
    B. I provide listeners with well-grounded facts.
    C. I get to the point quickly.
    D. I talk about my feelings and personal experiences.

14. When I am listening to someone:
    A. I like headlines vs. stories.
    B. I put myself in their shoes.
    C. I like it to have a logical flow and time for me to respond.
    D. I want to be inspired by their ideas.

15. In meetings I tend to:
    A. Insert facts and listen for next steps.
    B. Lead the conversation.
    C. I want everyone involved and people heard.
    D. Talk about the long-term possibilities.

16. When there is a pause in the conversation at lunch:
    A. I say something funny.
    B. I appreciate the time to gather my thoughts.
    C. I jump to a new topic.
    D. I ask how they are enjoying their meal.

17. I make people laugh by:
    A. Remembering funny past experiences with them.
    B. Making puns and witty one-liners.
    C. Telling a good joke that I've heard before.
    D. Sharing quirky characters that I've met.

18. In a meeting, I like to:
    A. Think before I speak.
    B. Take time to break the ice before getting to task.
    C. Be casual and playful.
    D. Be specific and stay on track.

19. I think people would say that my communication style is:
    A. Personal with a lot of give and take.
    B. Straightforward and active.
    C. Friendly and inspirational.
    D. Purposeful and informative.

20. I want the people who have conversations with me to:
    A. Understand the path forward and next steps.
    B. Feel like they are contributing something worthwhile.
    C. Have the most accurate information possible.
    D. Think of the opportunities open to them.

SCORING:

For each of the **20 questions** above, circle the letter that best describes your answer.

Question Number	Decisive	Animated	Methodical	Relatable
1	B	A	C	D
2	D	B	A	C
3	B	D	C	A
4	D	B	C	A
5	C	A	B	D
6	D	C	A	B
7	B	A	D	C
8	A	C	B	D
9	C	D	A	B
10	A	C	D	B
11	B	A	D	C
12	C	B	D	A
13	C	A	B	D
14	A	D	C	B
15	B	D	A	C
16	C	A	B	D
17	C	A	B	A
18	D	C	A	B
19	B	C	D	A
20	A	D	C	B
TOTAL:				

To use the scoring grid, go through each question and circle the letter that corresponds to your answer. Then add each of the four columns at the bottom of the grid.

Your "preferred" communications style is the column that has the highest score. You might find that you have similar scores in two of the styles, such as a 7 in one or a 6 in another. This is not unusual, and, with your self-report, you may find that you use two communication styles fairlyequally.

One caution: If you have a style score above 14 or 15, it might mean that you are overusing this style to the exclusion of others. A very strong score can become a weakness over time, which may seem counterintuitive. However, overuse limits your options, communication flexibility, and makes you very predictable.

Most of the time, one style will emerge as your preferred style. Read more for the descriptions of your preferred style and learn more about your strengths and areas of needed development.

Then you can review the other style descriptions and pay attention to the ways you can communicate more effectively with others who have a different style than yours.

Finally, this is a self-reported score that is quite accurate. However, we suggest that you have a colleague who knows you well and whose judgment you trust take this survey with you in mind. Comparing the scores can give you a "reality check" about how you are seen as a communicator.

The Communication Styles

Decisive

Decisive communicators are seen as independent, hardworking, and assertive, *in both their communication and leadership behavior*. While comfortable with abstract ideas and strategies, they are interested in discussing pragmatism most of all. They strive for clarity and efficiency in their communications, and they may tend to focus more on the goal then the details of getting there.

In their conversation, Decisives are fast talkers and can sometimes be overbearing. They quickly speak up about issues that are important to them and speak with confidence. They are strong-minded, even stubborn, and can be very determined. They pride themselves on getting things done and seeking closure. Accomplishing things is paramount for Decisives.

At the same time, Decisives will participate in an active debate and feel comfortable sharing their opinions freely. They will appreciate a different perspective as long as it is to the point and they can see the connections with what is being discussed. "Brainstorming" is not one of their strong points and they can get quickly frustrated with tangents and what they perceive as unrealistic ideas. Decisives tend to take action immediately after a decision is made.

A phrase you may hear a Decisive use: *"Git 'r done."*

Decisives prefer conversations that are:

- Planned well and thorough, with relevant information and limited small talk.
- Driven by solutions, not problems, preferably with several flexible options to discuss.
- Aligned with their goals, not their feelings.
- Practical and focused on results.
- Short and sweet.
- Free from jargon and platitudes.

Decisives **HATE** unfocused conversations that jump from topic to topic, without closure, or lack practicality.

Stress Communication Behaviors: In stressful situations, Decisive communicators tend to be *autocratic* and *controlling*. They are forceful and impatient with those who are perceived as unfocused. They may make snap decisions and shut down conversations about alternate or creative solutions. They may also be seen as overly competitive and domineering in conversations. They can interrupt others and not be aware of it.

Decisives may improve their communication effectiveness by:

- Being more mindful about not interrupting others or telling them what to do.
- Explaining their train of thought so others can understand the context of their opinion or decision, rather than blurting out the bottom line.
- Allowing time for spontaneous comments or questions about details.

- Taking a minute to pause and ask if their group has questions.
- Praising their team when they are doing a good job.

Some things to consider if you are in a conflict with a Decisive:

- Wait until they calm down. Remember, it's rarely personal or about you, although it might feel that way.
- Let them explain their side first. This reduces their anxiety about not being heard or understood.
- Write notes during the conversation, which may slow them down and allow you time to ask clarifying questions. This is an important thing to remember about working with Decisives. Taking notes allows you to pace the conversation because you can ask for clarification, allowing you to capture their ideas. They will like that you are interested in whatthey have to say.
- When giving your side, explain the facts briefly and calmly. Don't try to match their energy and stay in control.
- Think forward. Be prepared to offer several alternatives to the problem at hand. They love solutions.

Animated

Animated communicators (Animateds) have high-energy, are quite extroverted, and display a creative style and flair in their communication and behavior. They are witty and enthusiastic talkers, and use stimulating language to get their point across. They are not afraid to take risks, love to discuss big ideas, and are always looking forward. They tend to be optimistic and think about possibilities more than other people.

While naturally the center of attention in most groups and conversations, Animateds can be sensitive in their appreciation of others. They are natural cheerleaders who are inspired by opportunities.

They create positive environments through their playful discussion of possibilities from all sources. Animateds pride themselves on being peacemakers because of their high emotional sensitivity and openness. They persuade others through their superb storytelling and don't mind a spirited debate of ideas.

A phrase you may hear an Animateds use: *"Just thinking out loud here…"*

Animateds prefer conversations that have:

- Big, creative concepts and provocative questions.
- Ample time for socializing and sharing stories.
- New people or relationships.
- Upbeat and playful dialogue.
- Opportunities for praise for themselves and others.

Animateds **HATE** conversations that are too slow, rigid, or get bogged down in details.

Stress Communication Behaviors: In stressful situations, Animateds may become unfocused and unwilling to listen to practical matters. Although they may ask for a different opinion, often, they will not wait for the other person to finish. This is because they tend to become attached to unrealistic ideas and will not appreciate questioning or facts that do not support their assumptions.

Animateds may come across as over-confident and generalize when asked to back up a decision with data. If things are not going well, Animateds can sidetrack others by spending too much time on concepts and less on practical solutions.

Animateds may improve their communication by:

- Listening to and acknowledging facts. They can show this by taking notes in meetings.
- Being willing to accept criticism or talk about practical matters as they arise.
- Promising only what they can handle at the moment, and not taking on more than they can do in the excitement of the moment.
- Asking clarifying questions to show that they are listening to others. *This is really hard for them, but a skill they can develop.*
- Speaking concisely and sticking with one idea, and not trying to share all their thoughts and using expansive language.

Some things to consider if you are in a conflict with an Animated:

- Understand that they do not like conflict and may not speak rationally at times.
- Emphasize that the discussion is not personal, but about a specific issue that you need to resolve together.
- Be prepared to validate their side before explaining your own.
- Agree a way to move forward with specific answers. This works best after they feel heard.
- Have them repeat what you've agreed on to ensure that you've reached the same conclusion. It might be helpful to capture the agreements in notes and distributing them.

Methodicals

Methodical communicators (Methodicals) are detailed-oriented planners with excellent memories. Highly disciplined and reliable, they absorb data easily and are appreciated for their persistence and thoroughness in their work style, writing, and language. They are perceived as calm, rational, and formal in their speaking style.

Methodicals rely on experience and data as a conversational guide, logically following their knowledge to an airtight solution. They are excellent researchers, but they may not be confident in taking risks or stating opinions in meetings. They may mitigate that risk by asking open-ended questions that subtly point to their concerns.

They often seem reserved and are more comfortable in small groups. They are valued for breaking complex ideas into manageable and achievable parts. They are excellent at providing concise, constructive criticism, and reality checks in a team. Methodicals rehearse what they say, and they pride themselves on saying and doing things in the "right" way.

A phrase you might hear a Methodical use: *"Experience is the teacher of all things."*

Stress Communication Behaviors: Under stress, Methodicals are acutely aware of what might go wrong in an idea or plan. This may cause them to become rigid, competitive, and judgmental in what they say to others. Because of their cautious natures and reliance on tried and true methods, they may paralyze a process by asking a lot of detailed questions when confronted with a new situation. When this goes on for a while, Methodicals are seen as hesitant and indecisive.

Methodicals are naturally succinct talkers and they like to be in the right. They may shut down when they are contradicted, especially in large group settings.

Methodicals may improve their communications by:

- Being more willing to start conversations with what might work instead of what will not.
- Sharing their subtle sense of humor and appreciation for word play more often.
- Allowing space to talk about how the work of today impacts the future, or how their work impacts a larger picture.
- Addressing their frustrations when they arise in a calm and polite manner, so they don't linger.
- Asserting their need to analyze with confidence. They can do this by stating they need a specific amount of time (hour, day, etc.) to think and they will report back.

Methodicals prefer conversations that are:

- Based on fact and reason, not personal feelings or unrealistic ideas.
- Exhibit thorough preparation and conversation with a deep knowledge of the issue(s).
- Focused and concise, to the point, with clear next steps.
- Have ample time for questions about any suggested changes but may require set boundaries for more detailed discussions in a smaller group.
- Placed within a context that clearly defines their role, responsibilities and expectations.

Methodicals **HATE** conversations that wander off topic, use ambiguous language, or focus on feelings.

Some things to consider if you are in a conflict with a Methodical:

- They may be holding on to things you've forgotten about.
- They are uncomfortable speaking freely, so give them time to express themselves. Show that you are interested in what they have to say, but don't be pushy.
- Keep your voice even and measured.
- Back yourself up with rules, facts, or past experiences whenever possible.

- If a decision is required, be prepared to give them adequate time to think it through thoroughly. They don't like to be rushed or decide in the moment. The conversation may have to happen in two parts.

Relatable

Relatable communicators (Relatables) are people-oriented and focused on relationships. Natural diplomats, they are friendly, supportive, and cooperative. They are avid socializers who possess high emotional intelligence and understand people's feelings and motivations. They have a deep antipathy for conflict and may be hesitant to share their real perceptions, ideas and feelings because of this strong aversion.

Relatables often seek input and are expressive in their appreciation of others, making them sought out as open, calming, and gracious listeners. They are the ones who always remember your name and ask about your health and family. Relatables have generous senses of humor and are often seen as good sports, at times at their own expense. They are reliable but need clear communication around plans and stable environments to thrive. They like to feel appreciated for what they "bring to the table."

A phrase you might her a Relatable say: *"How can I help?"*

Relatables prefer conversations that are:

- Based on trust and transparency, and where it is safe to express feelings.
- Relatables like to understand context so they can consider how a situation may impact the other relationships they care about.
- Preferably with a group, rather than putting them on the spot.
- Reinforced with praise and respect.
- Moderately paced with ample time for everyone to express themselves.
- Seek input from everyone in the group. Inclusion is very important to them.
- Focused on achievable outcomes and clear next steps. Relatables like to meet the expectations of others.

Relatables **HATE** conversations that lack interaction or respect, with no eye contact, frequent interruptions, or personal criticism.

Stress Communication Behaviors: Relatables get stressed when they are confronted with sudden change, murkiness, or potential conflict. In these situations, they may become anxious andslow to speak in fear of doing or saying something wrong. Often, they will weakly agree in a group context, hiding their real emotions with a smile, rather than be assertive.

They may make passive-aggressive comments if they feel that they are going along with things that they don't believe in. Relatables may also take situations personally and respond impulsively, or they may blow up suddenly in a meeting or conversation because they have been holding on to their emotions. This can surprise others because they thought everything was fine.

They can be a little needy about feeling appreciated and acknowledged and will often seek feedback about their ideas in subtle ways.

Relatables may improve their communications by:

- Being willing to assert their opinions directly and in the moment, even if it may be uncomfortable. *This will be hard for them.*
- Setting boundaries around your availability at work for personal conversations, or letting others take credit for your efforts. Relatables are often the glue that holds a team together, but that may come at the expense of their time and productivity.
- Taking initiative around changes and replacing hesitancy with assertiveness by saying, "Let me think on that and get back to you in an hour/tomorrow, etc."
- Understanding that others do not place as much emphasis on emotions and bringing more facts and information into the conversation.
- Organizing your thoughts and rehearsing before you speak to a larger group.

Some things to consider if you are in a conflict with a Relatable:

- Because they work so hard to be sensitive to others, they may not be aware when their impact doesn't live up to their intent. They may not know that you have an issue with them.
- They will likely take criticism *very* personally and may shut down if they feel threatened or attacked.
- Be prepared to validate their feelings about the issue. Try and show real concern.
- Keep your voice even and measured and ask for help in working out a solution.
- If a decision is required, be prepared to give them adequate time to think it through thoroughly. The conversation may have to happen in two parts, because their emotions might be rather high and get in the way of making a thoughtful decision.

Summary

Understanding your communication style is an important element in every leader's portfolio. Developing the ability to be flexible and agile with other styles different that yours builds your resilience and effectiveness.

Using this survey to build your teams or work group's understanding of the different styles within the group is essential to high team performance (Sanaghan & Eberbach, 2013).

Good luck with your communication journey!

How to Review the S2P2 Communication Survey with Your Team/Group
A Team "Diagnostic" Meeting Design

The following will be a description of a team/group meeting design that takes what is learned from the S2P2 Communication Survey and discussing its implications for the team's overall performance going forward. (*In order to simplify language, we are going to use the term "team" todescribe groups.*)

It might be a good idea to have a trusted, *neutral* facilitator help debrief this diagnostic meeting, so the team leader can fully participate. The good news about this kind of meeting is that there really is no risk attached to it. People find that learning about themselves and others is interesting and educational. There are no winners or losers with this survey, just interesting information to digest.

This information sets the stage for a great conversation and, most importantly, some agreements about how to work together most effectively going forward. It is important to actually do something with this information and not let it be just an "interesting" experience.

We are going to assume that everyone on the team has taken the survey and they are willing to share their results with others.

1. The facilitator should plot everyone's scores on a flipchart or white board, with names attached so everyone can see how others scored. It might look like this.

Name	Decisive	Animated	Methodical	Relatable
Ann	7	3	6	4
Brad	4	3	10	3
Carl	4	4	4	8
Denise	3	9	4	4
Elizabeth	10	2	5	3
Frank	4	4	6	6

2. Each person should talk briefly about their scores and reactions to them (e.g. I was surprised. Right on target. Wow, I have a very strong score in Decisive. We seem to have a lot of Relatables on the team.)

    The goal here is just to get a conversation going and understand how people view their personal communication scores.

3. The facilitator may ask the team to complete the personal reflection questions that follow, asking one or two follow-up questions to get the team to start talking:

- Were there any surprises with the individual scores?
- As a team, what are your communication strengths? Were there any areas of needed development?
- Is there anything you need to be conscious about? (i.e., *We have a whole lot of Visionaries in our team, or lots of Relatables and not enough Decisives.*)

It is most helpful if the facilitator probes for implications such as:

- "Given that we have lots of Visionaries or Relatables, how does that influence our productivity as a team?"
- "How are our team meetings designed to be inclusive of all the different styles we have?"
- "Where could we get in trouble going forward?"

The goal here is to get some real ownership for the teams scores and thinking about their possible implications. This should be an easy conversation to have because you are not criticizing anyone, only seeking to understand each other, and how the different styles can influence (+ or -) team functioning.

4. Lastly, and this is only a suggestion, it might be helpful to generally agree on some *ground rules* or working agreements that would help the team be even more effective in the future.

The facilitator might say something like: "*Given our combined scores, what might be 2 or 3 ground rules that we can agree to and that would really help us build on our communication strengths and overall team performance?*" It would be helpful to suggest a couple of ground rules to start, for example:

- We need to make sure we design our future meetings to be inclusive of all the different styles we have. So far, we rely too much on our Decisive and Methodical styles.
- We seem to be missing an Animated style. We need to bring some peers into some from other teams to inform some of our important conversations to make sure we are looking at more possibilities and not rushing into action.
- We need to make sure that we hear from everyone in our team meetings. This way all the perspectives get shared before we make decisions that affect everyone.

Next Step

Going forward, using the "Cascading Meeting Design", we will create a set of meaningful ground rules. I will use eight team members as a working model for this meeting design.

XX   XX   XX   XX

1. The facilitator would ask participants to organize into pairs and create three "ground rules" or working agreements that would take the different communication styles in the group into consideration and build on the strengths of the groups. (5 to 6 minutes).

2. Then the facilitator would ask each pair to work with another pair (four people now) and share their three "ground rules" with each other. The goal for the larger group of four would be to "generally agree" on the very best three ground rules for the group. (8 to 10 minutes)

   Suggest that participants look for common ground ideas, because there will probably be some.

   Watch for "clumping", where people don't want to lose any ideas and put all ideas together in order to include everything. For example:

   > *We need to make sure we design our meetings to include all four communication styles, use active listening and make sure agendas are sentout ahead of time.*

   These are three different ground rules! You want to avoid this. Simple and clear ground rules are what you want. For example:

   > *We need to make sure that everyone gets a chance to talk in our team meetings.*

   > *We need to use more information and data with our decision-making, because we tend to wing it too much.*

   > *We need to decide upon the rules for important team decisions* (e.g. **who** makes **what** decision).

3. The facilitator would then take a suggested ground rule from each group of four, and capture the suggestions on a flipchart or white board. They would go around as many times as necessary to get all the ground rules written down in full view. You might have a total of six ground rules *(there tends to be a fair amount of overlap, so you often just get four)*.

4. Then give each participant two dot stickers to use as "votes" and indicate their favorite ground rules. What happens most often is that you end up with two or three that get the most votes. It is helpful to try and work with up to three ground rules, not five or six (Sanaghan & Eberbach, 2013).

5. Try the ground rules out for two weeks and then *anonymously*, assess their effectiveness to see if they need to be changed or enhanced.

Personal Reflective Questions

1. What is your strongest communication style?

    _____

    _____

2. What are three strengths your communication style brings to the table?

    1. _
    2. _
    3. _

3) Write down two or three examples of how your communication style has been effective in leading and managing people. Be specific.

    1. _
    2. _
    3. _

3. What is an area of your communication style that needs further development?

    _____

    _____

    _____

4. What other style(s) is most challenging for you to communicate with? Why do think this is?

    _____

    _____

    _____

5. Please identify three people with whom you communicate most often. Next to each person's name, try and identify their communication style. Do you see any patterns?

    1. _
    2. _
    3. _

6. What is one specific behavior you want to be more conscious of, regarding how you com-municate" (e.g. listen more, talk less, be more conscious of my impact on others, use more stories to convey my message).

    _____

    _____

References

1. Leadership on the Line. Ronald Heifetz and Marty Linsky (2017) (revised edition). Harvard Business School Press

2. The Practice of Adaptive Leadership (2009) Ronald Heifetz and Marty Linsky. Harvard Business School Press

3. The Decision to Trust. (2010) Robert F. Hurley. Jossey–Bass

4. Trust Rules (2017) Rob Lee. The Trust Lab

5. The Magic of Communication Styles (2016) Paul Endress. Cardinal House Press

6. 10 Communication Secrets of Great leaders (2012) Mike Myatt, Forbes magazine

7. Effective Communication and Leadership (2018) Leigh Anthony, Small Business Chronicle

8. Leadership is a Conversation, (2012) Boris Groysberg & Michael Slind, June. HBR

9. How to Build an Exceptional Team (2013) Patrick Sanaghan & Kimberly Eberbach. HRD Press

10. The Seduction of the Leader. (2016) Patrick Sanaghan &Kimberly Eberbach. Academic Impressions

11. Generating Buy-In: Mastering the Language of Leadership. (2004) Mark S. Walton

12. The Communication problem Solver: Simple Tools and Techniques for Busy managers (2010) Nannette Rundle Carroll

13. The Listening Leader; How to Drive Performance by Using Communicative Leadership. (2017) Zugaro & Zugaro. FT Press

14. Nonverbal Communication by Judee K. Burgoon, Laura K. Guerrero & Kory Floyd, (2016). Routledge

15. Administration 101: What do you have to do to Become a "Great Communicator"? (June 17,2018) David D. Perlmutter. The Chronicle of Higher Education

16. Why Leaders who Listen Achieve Breakthroughs. Elizabeth Doty. (March 21, 2016) Strategy & Business

17. COMPASS: Your guide for Leadership Development and Coaching (2017). Center for Creative Leadership. Peter Scisco, Elaine Biech & George Hallenbeck

www.ingramcontent.com/pod-product-compliance
Lightning Source LLC
Chambersburg PA
CBHW081540040426
42447CB00014B/3442